VIGIL

Vigil

Poems

Joseph Geskey

BROKEN TRIBE PRESS

Vigil

Copyright © 2026 Joseph Geskey
First Edition

Paperback ISBN: 9781965412121

Front cover art by Stacy Fabbre

Cover design by Jacob Arms

Published by Broken Tribe Press
Lawrence Landing Company
Raleigh, North Carolina 27609
USA, North America

Broken Tribe Press is a proud member of:

Independent Book Publishers Association
  and
Community of Literary Magazines and Presses

www.brokentribepress.com

BROKEN TRIBE PRESS

CONTENTS

III.

IV.

For Tara and Avery, again

Existentialism

It is not that life is meaningless.
Asthenia to faith while shivering
in winter, all that useless beauty
of austere trees and moonless nights
until the spark of light and warmth
from the discovery of combustion.
Life like two shy individuals,
let's call them hydrogen and oxygen,
on opposite sides of a gym floor
at a high school dance, thirsty
for companionship, finding one
another, their loneliness quenched.
Devoted to everything secular,
acolytes of daily experimentation
to life's unsolvable conundrums,
performing cardiopulmonary resuscitation
over the body even though it's futile.
At peace they did everything they could.

I.

Failing Better

Old coffee can, dipping into a stream,
trying to capture darting minnows,
my father watching, drinking beer.

Catching a few, transferring them
into a bowl when I returned home,
already planning to buy fish food

so I could prove to my parents
that I was responsible enough
one day to care for a dog.

Waking up distraught, finding
them dead, no explanation offered,
chlorinated tap water causing suffocation.

Hand on a hot stove parenting style.
Not one book in our home growing up,
dust motes on empty shelves, instead

tomes of knowledge found under the night sky
or the undercarriage of a late-model Chevy.
"*College boys*," he would frequently say.

McNamara's "Whiz Kids," CEO's
of financial institutions too big to fail,
book smart but lacking common sense.

The obviousness of *fail better*. Change
bait from night crawlers to shiners,
move locations, if your next meal is in doubt.

Last year of his life he became homebound
then increasingly bedridden before discovering
"Morphine makes dying easier."

Finally freed from being a suburban deer
struck by a car and suffering on the road,
back in a field, the charity of a bullet.

Childhood

*'We look at the world once, in childhood. The rest is
memory.'* –Louise Gluck

"*I have a good idea,*" my daughter
would say, & my wife & I
knew we couldn't imagine
what was going to come next:
fine art painting of a three-year-old.
Reams of recycled white paper
set down like a drop cloth on the floor,
traipsing muddy brown footprints
walking to where? Hand-squeezed
Elmer's glue to affix a handful of grass
& haphazardly placed twigs,
& I silently thought, no more bedtime
stories about the three little bears
huffing & puffing & blowing down houses.
Paintbrush clumsily spreading daubs
of yellow in an approximate circle
in the upper right-hand corner
with variegated blue streaks under it.
Her fine motor skills didn't do nuance yet.
"*Do you know what it is?*"
Post-truth philosophers would be laughed at
since the answer was clear:
"*It's Grammy's house,*" with a satisfied smile,
& no advanced techniques would ever
improve upon the joy of her vision.

What We Miss From Our Grandmothers

Days before the birds started
their southerly migration,
the ancient radiator
would cough, spit, and hiss heat
like a bronchitic smoker
after months of slumber.
Mid-morning, already hours
into her day, mixing eggs,
flour, and salt, her rolling pin
wielded as deftly
as a sculptor or painter,
a large sheet of rolled dough
would be cut into thin strips
and placed in a pot with carrots,
celery, chicken, and broth,
brought to succulence
after the whoosh of a match
lighting a gas stove.
Looking out the porthole
of a kitchen window,
spoken poetry of domesticity,
admonishing me to wear
a Soviet-style hat and coat
so I wouldn't "catch a cold."
Devotion to empiricism,
dazzling subatomic discoveries,
my daughter is home from school,
inpatient with illness, asking me
how she can feel better.

I go to the pantry, pull out
a can of chicken noodle soup
and place it in the microwave
for ninety seconds, knowing
she will not recover as quickly
as I did a half-century ago.

Grandmother

An elementary school education
Didn't allow her to praise
All that she loved with eloquence.
Struck mute, but still wondrous,
Eking out a ~~subsistence~~
Substantive existence.
Sinew to sinew, dust to dust,
Her gnarled hands like an oak
Tree's roots, where we would rest
Under the tent of its leaves
In the oppressive mid-summer sun
Laughing like we were illicitly stealing
Extra break time from a tyrannical boss.
How does someone get so good
Mending ripped jeans, knowing
When to use Mercurochrome
Versus Merthiolate for boyhood
Cuts and scrapes, and satiate
A ferocious hunger? Remembering
Picking gluttonous-sized tomatoes
From the fence line strip of garden,
It's natural au jus from thick slices
Saturating lightly toasted white bread
With a generous coating of butter,
Served with cold tap water.
Fifty years later, reflecting on
The antonyms: poverty, prosperity.

Being Called Soft as a Boy

A line of fathers and sons
stand on the crowded creek shore
casting fishing poles like fans
doing the wave at a sporting event.
Stocked trout, outdoorsman's Christmas,
without worrying about the time of day,
tackle, location, or cloud cover.
Embellished stories, hoping
that their sons will want to go
again at every possible opportunity.
The sudden tug of line startled me,
my father attempted to coach me,
nicotine-less for over an hour,
instructions louder and faster.
Eventually, I hold the fish
before it slips from my hands,
thrashing on the rocks
like a grand mal seizure,
and run away as he effortlessly
attends to its suffering.
Reliving this day as I turn my father
on his side before changing his diaper,
gently applying creams and ointments
to the weeping skin on his buttocks,
silently nodding to the ghosts
of my uncles calling me *soft*.

The Swimmers

The devoted ones are star pupils,
bent over at the starting block
at the call of *"Take your marks"*
& respond by launching themselves
up and outward after hearing the beep,
entering the temple of cerulean water
with steepled hands,
their legs propelling them
like an outboard motor
creating turbulence in its wake,
learning the math of Euclidean angles
as their arms maximize the efficiency
of their strokes while simultaneously
solving physics problems pertaining
to Newton's Three Laws of Motion.

Ten lane lines like a sheet of paper
where, like poets, the swimmers
compose an antibacchius metrical foot:
stroke, stroke, breath,
stroke, stroke, breath, ...
before finally touching the wall
and exiting the water,
looking at the time it took them
to finish their race,
& where in a few seconds
the only evidence of their performance
will have to be recorded in history
because the democracy of swimming
demands that time is erased
& the page of empty water starts anew.

Pediatric Psychiatric Crisis Center Located on Butterfly Garden Drive, Columbus, Ohio

The children here have already learned
that the stars in the night sky
are fixed & can't be pulled to earth,
laboring under the increasing strength of medication
desperately trying to escape the abiding,
cramped sadness of memories
filling the mind's vast landscape,
who hope & envy
the resilience of a one-gram butterfly
who decides to plan its liberation
after flittering repeatedly against
a glass window in a conservatory
before softly landing on a patron's brightly hued shirt
& gets through the butterfly garden's first door.
Seemingly discharged, it must now
confront the challenge of an anteroom
designed to anticipate a rogue butterfly
& is stymied before it can finally exit.
Looking out your window,
know that night hides
the introverted beauty of a small bunch
of urban wildflowers, persisting, like you,
hoping the grains of those pills
allow you to eventually soar
like a kaleidoscope
of unconstrained butterflies pollinating
every possible flower under light-filled skies.

The Mercy of Migration

Why a half-century later
from my childhood
do I watch a California Scrub-Jay
& its disheveled appearance,
cerulean feathers like it rubbed
haphazardly against a freshly painted
sky & think about grief?

Three boys allowed to stay outside
well into weekend summer nights,
where we never missed the start
of the 8:40 PM fireflies' performance.

Hearing the bird's constant shrieks
reminds me of how we used to
trash talk one another.
Wondering too if it may be a sentinel,
keeping vigil for any predators.
How we would look out for one another
if one of us might be in trouble.

Learning how the birds conduct funerals
by shrieking for up to thirty minutes
over the body of a dead jay,
who otherwise would go unnoticed.
How the birds don't migrate
no matter the harshness of circumstances.
Unlike me, how I couldn't wait to leave home.

Thinking now that Tolstoy was wrong.
Yes, the three of us happy together
in our own little clique
but my two friends & their families
were similarly unhappy:
Heroin overdoses taking them both,
& the small mercy they received
after I left: not to be reminded
of this every time they saw me.

Ghazal for the Sleepless Children

The loud sounds past bedtime that distort sleep:
It's only thunder, honey; you need more sleep.

I can hear the crickets and cars racing outside.
We'll close the window; you can't ignore sleep.

The car horns and fireworks woke me up.
Just this once, our team's winning dwarfs sleep.

All that noise from the neighbors next door.
They had an argument; you need your sleep.

I heard popping sounds and got scared.
The police are outside, it's safe to sleep.

The explosions seem to be coming closer.
Come, *Hayati*, there will be no more sleep.

Daily prayers for the return of quiet nights
and the anxious generations who mourn sleep.

Is the answer to teach them to count sheep?
For some, infinity will arrive before postwar sleep.

On Overhearing a Conversation
about Mama Bears

His approach is unhelpful,
No concierge service to skip
The lines of the afflicted

Or donation levels for secret
Access that's unavailable for others.
Piqued by rage and punishing weights,

As if disease is an intruder
Intimidated by brawn and violence.
Self-pity fueled by liquor,

Insomnia of dueling debates,
Cursing genetics and God,
There is no dramatic arc

Of hostage negotiation
Where illness will trade
One individual for another.

In the wild, mama bears
Seek to protect their cubs
By living closer to humans

Because of male bears fear
Of them. Preternatural ear
for empathy of lived experience,

giving children needed resources
to be able to bear hardship
under their careful watch,

they may sprinkle hemp seeds
into their children's food
because of their own research

to complement the treatment
plan given by strangers
in white coats, vouchsafed

by their mothers to whom
they crawl up next to whenever
they are fearful and don't understand.

My Sixth Grader Asks Me Why She Has to Learn About Mesopotamia

Because they are teaching her
how to prepare for the diaspora
to adulthood and leave the protection
of home. The need to evolve from
the Keatsian negative capability
of experiencing that first taste
of what she learned to call *apricot*
is more than ten-thousand years old.

The resilience of its fruit, transported
over millennium of blood-soaked lands.
The misconception that countries
have a fixed geography but rather exist
vicariously through the whims of its rulers.
How the grace of predictable harvests
of grain and fruit and the trust of trade
was not enough for those who wanted more.

How writing developed from cuneiform,
where pictures were representational
and somehow the concept of *more*
evolved into conquest and the resultant
language of the conquered were left
on their own, standing defenseless, armed
with nothing but reason or pleading
to overcome the latest in war innovation.

Thousands of years from her lesson
The House of Wisdom was destroyed.
So many books thrown into the Tigris
that it reportedly turned black with ink.
Acknowledgement that civilizations
don't survive on hoping the decibels
of prayers reach benevolent Gods.
And through each excavated body

we find that even though our skulls
are larger, the DNA extracted from bones
highlight we have more similarities
than differences, and while I empathize
with my daughter over how much
more she had to learn than I did,
I hope she and her classmates recall
more fragments before it's forgotten.

Marshmallow Test

He lived his childhood
believing everything
within a container
must be rationed.

He was obedient.
Carafe of water
beckoning thirst
while playing taught

temperance, foregoing
the indulgence of those
with a non-scarcity mindset,
water greedily guzzled

until quenched, then poured
over faces and bodies
before evaporating
without a second thought.

Imagination as big
as a canvas, learning
to thin his brushstrokes,
one-time allocation

of a few primary colors
that still settled below
the top of plastic palette
wells with so many unfilled.

Decades later he learned
about the marshmallow
experiment. If preschool

children could wait
fifteen minutes without
eating a marshmallow
placed in front of them
they could have two.

Unrealistic he thinks,
only in research labs
could a promise like this
be made and kept.

All the Things We Miss

Looking at a fresh snow-covered field
from afar and dismissing any possible interest
by labeling it cold and barren, while a mother
is frantically sniffing a fresh sheet of tracks,
incomplete sentences that might lead her
to a narrative of rediscovery.

Watching a convoy of bees,
winged migrants, using black light vision
to discover untapped pollen from stray wildflowers
that look like end-of-the-season leftovers,
tending them with such interest that next year
they may be picked for a bridal bouquet.

Recognizing within the corpus of Romantic poetry
Nature also inspires the Darwinists,
publishing their findings after walking
the same sheets of snow with empiric vision,
discovering coyote tracks and a trail
of blood droplets from his captured prey.

Hearing church bells among the secular
cacophony of sounds that command immediate
attention with a daily schedule violently tapping
on a wristwatch reminding me I am late,
transporting me back to a bell my mother would ring
when it was time to come home and eat and then run.

Dad and Daughter Day

Last few months before the teenage years,
anticipating it like you were approaching
the life expectancy from a terminal diagnosis.
Dad and Daughter Day, still willing
to be seen in public with a developing fossil,
wishing she was a slave to fashion,
especially if expected hemline lengths
are forecasted to be six inches longer this year.
Self-aware enough to not even comment on
why does someone so young have a daily skin
regimen more complicated than open heart surgery.
Two days before our date, I rupture a cyst
behind my knee after performing the heroic feat
of getting up out of my chair, wise enough
to not compare the pain to childbirth,
but wincing every time I take a step.
Unspoken words of maybe we should cancel,
before rummaging through the medicine cabinet
and find two nearly empty bottles of my father's
pain medicine five years after his death.
"*Thanks, Dad,*" I think, and how the word
 transcends the corporeal, never becoming extinct.

What I Hope My Daughter Learns

To watch an osprey survey
the Atlantic and then dive
sixty feet before pulling out
a fish on its first attempt
and not take a selfie afterward.
Quickly picking up a pill
from the floor before the dog
ingests it, because he has learned
that everything that comes
from your hand is joy.
Coming back home with a cut
over your knee after trying
something new, trying to staunch
the bleeding, cleaning the wound,
recognizing you need more help
and getting a few stitches.
Years later, looking at the scar
and smiling long after I am gone.

The Resonance of Seashells

She wants to share the ocean with you,
dipping her cupped hands into the water
until it overflows but arrives empty-handed.
Her first lesson, the importance of gestures.
She spends the next several hours building
sandcastles near the shoreline, waking up
the following day to see it washed away
by the moon's gravitational pull over the tides.
A second lesson, where extracting a pinky
promise not to destroy her kingdom
from an annoying older brother doesn't eliminate
the necessity of learning the equations
from unseen forces critical for success.
Her curiosity is rewarded when she finds
a conch shell on the beach and brings it home.
Told by her mother that you can hear the ocean
when you bring it to your ear. Years later,
a final lesson settling her mother's estate,
the shell still carefully wrapped in a storage box,
the resonance of what remains
                              and what is lost.

II.

A Honeybee Confronts a Threat

Admiring the discipline of a honeybee
armed with only one stinger
to deploy against potential threats,
surveying the garden of herbs,
sunflowers, and calendula
in a postcard-pretty suburb,
carrying payloads of pollen
through a nectar corridor,
before launching a stinger
into my arm, self-immolating
herself into oblivion,
stunning me into the realization
I am not so innocent.

Getting Older

"...The marriage / not the month's rapture."
Jack Gilbert, "The Abnormal Is Not Courage"

Maybe it's the instinct and impulse
of immediate gratification that nature
cautions us against. Eliot's withered
hyacinths perfuming trash, or Thomas
raging like a man looking for a fight
in the dying of the light. Outdoor hikes
through fields of bunch grass always
taking the same route. *Spalding's catchfly,*
it's demure white star-shaped flowers
in bloom after a season of dormancy.
Not interested in becoming peacock feathers
of colorful petals in landscaped gardens,
or to be pulled from the ground and chosen
to be part of the bridal bouquet. Demonstrating
what scientists call *negative senescence,*
improving survival as the plant ages,
its genes determined to experience sun
and wind until infinity, and what it feels like
to be both simultaneously warm and cool,
unlike us, who suffer the ravages
of cellular insurrection, the beneficial
stubbornness of growing deep roots.

Sorry For Your Loss

AI-written condolences won't console
a gutted heart, nor eliminate the menu
of where to sit and surveil
the incoherence of pain and loss.
Cherish those who stand in silence
with you and still send a signed sympathy
card pulled from a clearance sale stack,
old enough to realize it's the gesture that counts.
The blackbird sitting on a cherry tree, cold
April rain, not calling out in harsh belligerence
but rather busking in song, alone.
The fifty-year-old peony, dying back
into the earth and then resurrecting
its bloom. *Because we will never be
what the field remembers*, the fingerprints
of the hands that planted it have become a myth
in the subsequent generation that has been born,
a heavily redacted biography of displaying
a framed picture of the departed loved one
doubling as a memorable aphorism.

Sirens, Birdsong, and Church Bells

Praise a mother's incantation
that refuses to be silenced
by skin, tissue, muscle, or viscera,
propagating through a sea of amnion
before reaching fetal ears, forging
neural connections built with love
and whose child might grow up
one day to sing of injustice in a pitch
like an ambulance siren approaching
a beloved neighbor's house, keeping
people from getting back to sleep
in the type of neighborhood that convenes
in church pews on Sunday mornings,
where outside the riot of birdsong
attempts to disrupt the quiet prayers,
the parishioners thinking it contributes
to a picture-perfect Sunday instead
is evolution's bid to stave off extinction.

STEM as Part of a Flower

Night sky of wonder before learning
physical laws governing its existence
after being encouraged to wish upon a star
as an impressionable child. Newton's Law
diminishing the pull of heavens
but introducing us to the force of attraction.
First generation college students exposed
to Keats' *blushful Hippocrene* in a dying
manufacturing town, blue-collar parents
wondering how this helps their kids thrive
in the Anthropocene. The learned professions
striving for precision down to the subatomic world.
Every living thing taking a turn pithed on a table,
an autopsy only able to answer cause of death.
For now, a local meadow remains undeveloped,
no generals wargaming its strategic importance.
A colony of honeybees pollinating goldenrod,
lavender and bee balm, their stingers sheathed,
a sudden memory of when you first tasted
honey, intuitively grasping negative capability,
the repeated "*mmm*" with every bite.

Anyone Can Be Successful
If They Try Hard Enough

Bromides of self-reliance
From men and women
Where every time they came home
The dog's tail was waving
Like a child with a sparkler,
Extravagance of leftover
Dinners after having a choice
In deciding what the rest
Of the family would eat.
Library-quiet table where
They worked on homework,
Unlimited access to the expertise
Of their mom or dad
Without any bureaucracy.
Walking into a store,
After saving all summer
From the abundance
Of jobs they could choose from,
And buying their first audio
Equipment, finding out
The manufacturer raised
The price, only to have
Their grandmother hand
Them the remaining balance.
CGI trick of memory,
Pretending they were high wire
Artists, plying their craft
Without a safety net.

Thinking of this working
In an impoverished area
And listening to a woman
Tell me she was given drugs
By a sexually abusive father
Since the age of nine,
Mind daily transporting her
To the eye of a Category 5
Hurricane, tentatively
Celebrating a year of being clean.

Philosophy of *The Quick Brown Fox*

The quick brown fox jumps over the lazy dog.
High school typing class trying to accumulate
as many mistake-free words in a minute
under the teacher's panopticon gaze,
checking you didn't look down at the keyboard,
as if a quick glance at the letters were glimpses
of nudity when you promised not to look.
If shop class could be compared to philosophy
then so could typing, a more humane factory,
workdays spent over rhythmic clicking keystrokes,
the benefits of office work over manual labor
& all those broken bodies forced into early retirement,
while dreaming of Keynes fifteen-hour workweek.
Forty years later, typing my father's obituary
in templated form, errorless and efficient,
saving precious minutes so I can fall less behind
on checking off life's ever expanding to do list,
I light a candle in his memory and think about
the assembly-line of workers centering wicks
in machine-poured candles before they get lidded,
wondering when automation will perform that task.
A majority of workers forced to practice Stoicism
while the few with security enjoy eudaimonia.

House Call

Amid a field's amber waves
of grain rippling like a flag
in rural Ohio, a piano sat
like a desk in a trailer, piled
with pill bottles and papers.
An elderly woman paused
to catch her breath saying,
"I know I did this to myself."
Decades of smoking
to quell daily anxieties,
worried about others' tribulations.
An ash-filled empty beer can.
Once a gospel pianist,
she wanted God to know
her silence was due to infirmity
rather than a lapse of faith.
"I can read sheet music
but can't understand
what's written on my papers."
After hearing her play
a decades-old recording
of her music, I kneel
beside her as a supplicant
and show her how to use
her inhalers more effectively.
Discovering I was Bartimaeus,
finally seeing after so many years.

Still Life with Oranges

Van Gogh's six oranges
sit in a basket painted
in his familiar brushstrokes,
the striking yellow sunlight
in Arles-sur-tech, France
should have its own named color.
But we should gravitate
to the artist who learns
still life by painting
a once-varnished table
where a chipped, discolored
ivory bowl sits depressingly empty
while perfectly capturing
the sallow sunlight refracted
through soot-stained windows.
Imaging apophatic orbs of oranges
overhanging the rim of the bowl
because his family is hungry
& doesn't have the luxury
of unlimited time to perfect
his technique. And from desire
captures what it would be like
to be allowed to choose one
& imprint a thumbnail
before peeling the skin off,
the rind like a discarded garment,
before lifting it to a mouth
while the teeth puncture
the skin, a necklace of citrus
droplets spritzing the stagnant air
with overwhelming abundance
what we thought was impoverished.

The Misuse of Data

Data's ekphrastic beauty—
able to create pictures
from plotting individual stories.

On the x-axis is life satisfaction—
bliss as far as the eye can see.
On the y-axis are critical variables:

food, housing, employment, companionship,
each one a step to an easier climb
where cells don't age as rapidly

and the fight-or-flight hormones
remain safely tucked in their cells
with concierge level services

administered by former cruise ship
and Disneyland employees.
But on the lower rungs

there is an ambitious son
caring for a cancer-ridden mother
while others go off to college.

A daughter who is hostage to voices
trying to harm her and the ransom
demanded by health care will not be met.

Rather than looking to flatten
the imposing mountain slope,
biographers and politicians celebrate

the heroism of the individual,
overlooking the implicit accusation,
"If s(he) did it, why can't others?"

Forgetting about the decimal
sitting before a series of zeroes
before you reach that lonely one.

The cognitive dissonance that arises
when we focus on the one rather than grieve
over the exponential who have fallen.

Playing in Pain

Daily life like aging veteran athletes
who should have retired already—
hobbled by knee injuries, bad backs
& carpal tunnel syndrome.
Bosses like irascible head coaches & owners
who remind them how they are losing
on the scoresheet of profit margin.
They haven't been a star for decades
& know they are replaceable.
"Hey Doc, can you patch me up,
I need to get back out there,"
so they brace & tape themselves,
grab a handful of pills to make
the pain a little more bearable
while trying to keep their blood pressure
& cholesterol from further injuring them.
They are the metaphor of all heart now,
arriving early for their next shift,
the employee parking lot entirely full.

The Gift of Certain Fathers

It is an act of love,
how fathers reverse
the narrative technique
of show, don't tell.
Gifting an inheritance
of life lessons--
How the present
is the past, is the future.
There is always a there
but right now, there is a here.
Practice tithing, fasting,
and making promises,
so you know how it feels
to be poor, hungry
and disappoint others
so it doesn't hurt as much.

But we are obstinate.

The poet who writes on scrap
paper, because the puppy
and the toddler laugh at plans,
getting her poems accepted
ten times less than the worst
hitter in professional baseball,
who still won't quit.
The choreography of church
where we stand, kneel and sit
hoping our attendance counts

for something since there will be
no immediate reward.
A wide receiver running
his first crossing route,
ball spiraling toward his hands
reaching out, getting ready to pull
it against his chest before getting
hit at twenty miles an hour
and seeing neurological stars,
unfathomable headache,
and the hours of vomiting,
but coming to practice the next day
knowing there is always someone
willing to replace you.

Coming Up Sevens

Cool coffee, coagulated,
the last few sips before third
shift starts, tasting tobacco
leaves in everything. Three packs
a day, trying to hide her habit
from her mom, whose grandson
smells like he's the one smoking.

Monotonous factory line,
tobacco bander for down
market brands, not one smoked
to celebrate a marriage
or a new baby, but palliate
middle-class anxiety, cheaper
and easier than barbiturates.

Incumbent shifts of caring
for her bed-dependent mother
despite two hardy brothers.
Twice falling asleep coming
home from work in the morning,
saved by prescient engineers
designing wide grassy medians.

Two-hour bus rides to casinos
filled with oxygen tanks
and wheelchairs. Roll of quarters,
supplemented by what was left
over at the end of the month
from a modest pension and
buying processed foods in bulk.

Was she lucky at the slots
you ask? Think of Bishop's poem.
One day receiving a call
from my father's uninflected
voice stating, *"Your mother's dead."*
Scat from birds draped like
a necklace over her headstone

at the edge of a shade tree,
cleaning it off, noticing
the sun's rays like watch hands
pointing to an hour marker
as if viewed from above.
Time. What if she realized
after visiting departed

loved ones, the slow suicide
of wearing her life to the tread
knowing there were no parts left
to replace, so that her son,
young enough to understand
and do something meaningful
before it suddenly runs out?

Otherwise Unremarked Upon
Acts of Courage

A child afraid of monsters
looking with her mother
under the bed & in closets,
being brave by lying in bed
without a night light or asking
to sleep in her mother's bed,
a first reminder she is alone.

A woman seeing her ex-
drug dealer, offering
a liquidation-like sale
to obtain her business again.
Body & mind working together,
filing legal briefs to the Supreme
Court of the mind, being told
"You deserve this for your efforts."
The body in increasing pain
like a black site interrogation,
forcing herself to walk away,
not wanting to advertise
how much she was tempted.

A family man, kids in college,
wife with a chronic illness,
crawls under the belly
of twenty-year-old cars,
saving their drivers
several hundred dollars a month

for a new car they can't afford,
while his back, knees, hips,
shoulders, &wrists
amplify the pain to let him
know enough is enough.
Five more years to go
before full Social Security benefits,
he swallows a handful of pills
& leaves for work,
a coin flip as to whether fate
will comport with his plans.

The Stories of Long Winters

First snow of the year,
a fresh sheet of paper,
another year to craft
a story of transformation.
Late November through March,
storms add pages to the notebook
for extra encouragement.
Occasional epiphanies
between helping a mother
refill her weekly pill planner,
the snap-on lids unable
to be fully closed this year,
and sharing carpool duties
for ice hockey practice.
Chastising yourself over
your math skills, unable
to explain algebra to your child,
shelling out money, gas, & time
for a tutor, needing to pick up
extra shifts to cover the inflation
of expectations, practicing
the advice of "*Show, don't tell.*"
Tracks of footsteps rubbed
down to the earth despite
a foot of snow, erasure marks
from all the false starts,
consoling yourself again
"*There's always next year.*"

The Rising Price of Oranges

He read about the provision
of oranges and lemons
given to sailors to prevent scurvy
in History and Economics class.

Learned to match $C_6 H_8 O_6$
to Vitamin C in Chemistry,
and painted them sitting together
in a wicker basket as still life.

Future engineers approximated
their size and relationship on paper
as if creating a life-like reproduction.

The creatives played with shade
and color to create a narrative
harkening back to a child handling
an orb of fruit, making a connection
to the story *Good Night Moon*.

Our perspectives hardened
from those early years,
making a choice and picking a team
whether you knew it or not.

Late in life, partner sleeping,
delicately peeling the skin
from an orange, its silk-like pith
barely concealing the fruit
before taking it in your mouth,

and after finishing it
worrying about all the ways
they can become scarce
from climate change or war,
eventually becoming extinct.

In Praise of the Common Yarrow

The yarrow was my childhood flower.
The perennial battle between aphids
and spittlebugs versus wasps and hoverflies
had a decisive winner one summer:
a field filled with white flat-topped flowers,
providing shelter and nectar for both the winged
and the wingless. Good enough for Achilles
to carry into battle to treat wounded soldiers
by compressing crushed leaves against wounds.
The stalks of the plant could also be used
for divination and to serve as protection.
Hung over a doorway, or loosely strewn
in the shape of a cross on the steps
before walking into my house, I prayed
my father wasn't drinking, prepared just in case.

Self-Reflection on an Elevated BMI

Wrestling your own personal demons
prevents you from criticizing the haggard,
destitute man carrying a cardboard
message of *need* at an urban intersection,
long erased from being properly seen
as a neighbor, friend, & family member.

Conviviality of a businesswoman
at an after-work party, drinking enough
to quiet self-flagellating voices knowing
she will be standing in line when the bar
opens the next morning on her day off,
her luck of hanging on coming to an end.

Now you, clothes grappling your arms,
legs, & torso, the decades of expected
subservience you have demanded
from groaning joints & overworked organs,
treating the mind like a prodigal son
indulging its every grievance & excuse.

Food the drug of choice that binds you
with those suffering from other addictions.
Behind your back, some will substitute
gluttony instead of *ghrelin*. How judgment
always arrives before understanding
& the grace-starved need of forgiveness.

The Ozempic Poem

Inject two milligrams beneath
The skin every week because
You are—fill-in-the-blank reason.

The riddle of contemplating
The weight of everything lost
Staring at these empty hands.

Asphyxiation from adipocytes
Compressing the trachea,
No mercy, let alone forgiveness.

Empathy for smokers temporarily
Removing nasal prongs of oxygen
So they can still puff a cigarette.

The dignity of not questioning
Someone in withdrawal asking
For money to *"get something to eat."*

Although my veins are pristine
Pinch of skin, needle entering,
I am not close to being clean.

III.

Liminality

A second-grade girl calls out,
"We believe in you,"
When an opposing team's batter
Struggles to hit a pitch
Thrown from a coach a few feet away,
Her mom telling me
How excited she was to receive
First Holy Communion a few hours ago,
Saying, *"I want to taste Jesus,"*
& her joy when he hit the ball.

Thinking of the letters a soldier
Would send home, consoling
& reassuring his loved ones,
Unsure if he would read a response.
How his occupation changed
From farmer, teacher, student
To soldier, now facing a binary choice:
You or me, Us or them, instead
Of a Venn diagram between neighbors
If they met on a different landscape.

The inability to describe suffering.
How pacificism is not inviolable,
Watching a deer skidding across
A road onto a grassy median
After being struck by a car,
& the thrashing of its legs
As it tries to get upright

Watching its panic-stricken eyes,
Wishing for the mercy of a gun.
The doe's companions moving on.

My father in hospice care.
Aides using pillows to touch
His shoulders & turn him on his side
While they removed his diaper
& cleaned him, compassionately wasteful
In applying lotions & creams,
While I was hoping for a generous error
In his morphine dose to speed up
The appointment when the chaplain said,
"Soon he will be with his maker."

The Subversion of Michelangelo

During the Renaissance
Michelangelo dissected bodies
snatched from graves,
discovering the vessels,
muscles, & bones that power
our voyage through life
& published his discovery
on the ceiling of the Sistine Chapel
where *The Creation of Adam*
depicts God & the angels
transported in a vessel shaped
like the cross-section of a brain,
God & Adam reaching out
to one another, agonizingly
close, but never touching.

A Census Taking of the Believers

Matthew is the example.
Moth & rust destroy,
thieves steal on Earth.
The limits of language
accompany the vigil of loss.
Day's end, edge of sky,
purplish explosion caught
like a romantic still image
advertising elsewhere.
Thick coats of rust
on abandoned metals
in weed-infested yards,
a reliable calendar
like the annual rings
of an oak tree.
No undiscovered riches
sifting through one another's
possessions in seasonal
neighborhood yard sales.
Spoken narratives
of daily experience,
black and white,
simple cause & effect,
means to an ultimate end.
Devotion to the sacraments,
seeing the impermanence
of earthly attention, faith
rewarding a better eternity.

The Last Shall Be First

Where is the proof?
I think of a leopard
trailing behind a pair of hyenas
for the opportunity to reclaim
an antelope they have stolen
without a concern for ethics.
The day before Christmas
a mother, after saving
her denarii for an entire year,
hopes to scavenge a few
last minute deals at a mall
to give the illusion of abundance.
Well-dressed parishioners
at Midnight Mass, setting out
plates of cookies, milk, and carrots,
safe under Canon and Common law,
while others build their resilience
strength training under hunger
and anxiety, multiples more
than ten thousand hours spent
to finish first at their passing.

Potential Energy

The hand: curled into a fist,
extended in friendship,
raising an open palm
to protest groupthink,
clapping so hard until it hurts,
receiving a high-five,
steady while the index finger
repeatedly presses a trigger,
cramping in restraint while trying
to dress an open wound
without causing further pain,
the soft brushing motion
over the curves of a body,
and because God can't lend
one to help those who have fallen,
mine haven't been steepled
since childhood.

The Seasons of Mass Shooting

Clouds of exhaust pour from tailpipes
idling at stoplights in December, while snow clouds
rise spontaneously as wind shakes
oak and maple branches bare.

The sun disinfects rather than warms,
sharpening the mind—
what was once unknown is now a known known:
calculable odds of surviving
multiple mass shootings.

Locked doors.
Closed blinds.
Dog barking, anxious.
Looking straight ahead in public
as if wearing a cervical collar.

A great-grandparent watches a Spotted Turtle
emerge from a still pond with a child in May
who must pass through metal detectors
to learn, while she remembers
Bert the Turtle teaching her what to do
in case of an atomic bomb in the 1950's:

He'd duck and cover, duck and cover,
He'd hide his head and tail and four little feet
He'd duck and cover!

The child's first question is about survival:

How can the turtle survive when it's so slow?

There are no legislators in the wild
to protect American Robin eggs
from a gang of crows.

While the child blows out a candle
and prepares to say her evening prayers,
I think how far, and through how many languages,
that elegy has traveled—
and all the poems still to come
from grief.

Before We Become Ghosts

Aging begins to turn us into apparitions.
Praise the American robin who flits
among the vertical bare branches
of a backyard Tatarian maple tree
on this anonymous late autumn day
as if she is strumming the strings of a guitar,
singing a song for an audience of one.
Reminding us the show must go on.

Obituaries of the Anonymous

I think of the anonymous men
           and women who spend late nights
                        working
on the upper floors
           of Chicago buildings,
                    occasionally
startled by the sound
           of a passerine crashing into
                    an office
window. After forty years
           of death by skyscraper, researchers
                    accumulated
enough bodies
           to measure tarsus, wing, and beak,
                    and concluded
that during this time
           the birds have become smaller in size
                    but have longer
wingspans. Profundity
           of a few grams and centimeters
                    so they can sing
together
           as a band of inveterate troubadours
                    traveling to Florida
on tour in Winter,
           and where a child will see and hear
                    the wings and songs

of warblers
and never forget that particular day.
I wonder how many of
them,
when they retire, will move to Maine
and stand on the side of the
road
with the tourists watching a moose
in a field, marveling at its size
and presence, and will have enough
time to revisit the same spot
a few years later, after the moose
has died, and where eagles,
vultures
bears and wolves feasted
on its carrion, while the
termites
and beetles patiently waited their turn.
Berry plants and thistles in
bloom
from the outline of the moose
and the work of funeral-
goers,
this wild beauty that stuns
one into silence so he can better
describe the awe of returning
back
to
the earth.

The Big Dipper

The insomniac sits alone
on the front porch looking
at the night sky for relief
from earthbound anxieties
& locates The Big Dipper,
associated with a funeral
procession in Arabic folklore.
He spots an oriole departing
a maple tree under the star
of Merak, the bottom edge
of the bowl before flying
in a parabola to Dubhe
at the top edge, then reaching
Megrez in a straight line,
flying parabolically again
to the distant tip of the handle,
Alkaid, descending to Amizar,
then Alioth, & through Megrez
to Phecda before returning
home under the light of Merak.
I give praise to the oriole
for allowing me, in my sixth decade,
to retrace the stars in the night sky
& create the symbol of infinity
despite the increasing reminders
of senescent cells & the laws
of gravity that thins out prayers,
& why we need poets wandering
with pastors, physicists, & astronomers
late at night searching among the stars.

Vigil

Every real intimacy includes its end.
Late night vigils over the body
when we were young, gorging
ourselves on the bacchanalia
of intimacy and pleasure, wondering
when abundance became boredom
as we contemplate its coming erasure
and remain to attend to its burden.
Having given ourselves over
to empiricism and the experience
of generals leading a supposed war,
who marshal rounds of chemotherapy
to quash a cellular uprising
leaving the body ravaged
and who never want to surrender.
Experiencing how suffering transforms
from a secular to faith-based definition:
Desert-parched lips brushed with water,
wafer of narcotic placed under
a penitent tongue, performing
ablutions of an incontinent body,
receiving plainsong prayers of loved ones
from matins to vespers until our negation.

Ode to the Liver

And the citizenry of hepatocytes
who unceremoniously labor
within bodies that have become
like the engine room of the Titanic.

Sorely underrepresented in the pantheon
of works that champion muscles,
heart, and brain, and when mentioned,
is usually as the cause of death of its author.

The quiet men and women sitting
alone and silently listening
to memory's voices relaying
a queue of unremitting grievances.

Each liver cell a biographical anecdote
accompanied by a drink, one after another.
Self-interrogated by a law-and-order psyche
that ignores the Double Jeopardy Clause.

Appeals to a higher court have been denied.
A boy unable to stop his father from hitting
his mother, a mother hoarding every possession
because she can't handle another loss...

Inflamed and cirrhotic cells, decades past
the grace of tolerance, buttressed
by the genetics of parents and torments
they also kept buried within themselves.

Reflecting on those late nights spent in silence
while internal confessions poured forth,
the accumulating obituaries of people
who you wanted to reach a denouement with.

Near the end of life pay homage
to the hepatocytes who served as janitors,
bail bondsmen, and fixers while its employer
prayed and played the lottery,

hoping in vain for a different outcome.

Time to Say Goodbye

Wind-strewn and swirling yellow
Honey locust leaves litter
The street like a ticker tape
Parade, celebrating a lunch hour
Without a call from the nurses
Saying my father's pain has worsened.
Shingles of leaves have begun
Their slow collapse off the rooftop
Of Sycamores, soon unable to protect
The winged or wingless from the elements.
Blighted backyard European Beech
And its withered, curled, leathery leaves
That once stood sentinel every summer
Providing us with an awning of shade
To linger and laugh into the night.
It's past time to say goodbye, knowing
The charity of collecting another day
Further decimates the destitute
Who have nothing further to give.

Sunday Mornings

"The boy needs religion,"
 My grandfather demanded.
The only time I remember
Spending time alone with him,
Sunday mornings dropping me
Off at a Roman Catholic Church
Before attending his Russian Orthodox one.
Picking me up after Sunday school
Asking me what I learned,
Imperceptibly nodding afterward.

A half-century later, at the time
The faithful are getting ready
For Mass, I sit watching
My yard-filled shadows slowly
Being overcome by the movement
Of the sun yielding a light
Where everything can be examined,
Viewing these few precious hours
Not as a chance to accrue more
Billable hours, nor as a legislator
Making false bonhomie
Attempting to accumulate power.

Instead, I want to be Diogenes
On the receiving end of Alexander the Great
Asking him what he wished for,
Stunned to hear him say,
"Only for you to get out of my sun,"

So I can resume my search for solace
Finding the right words in the right order,
Experiencing the burning of days
From the calendar of my life,
Taking it salvifically to my grave.

The Right to Remain Silent

Doesn't exonerate us
in a jury comprised
of our better angels,
pleading the fifth amendment
against self-incrimination
of all the acts we failed to commit.

The fissile material of language
violently launched to harm,
earworms into memory
adding to history's grievances
we pretend not to hear.

False grace of stoicism
when the executive function
of the brain wordsmiths
an anodyne response
or retains risk-averse lawyers
who counsel the butterfly effect
of any type of involvement.

Meanwhile a potential community
of Good Samaritans stand idly by
while someone chokes to death.

Suburban neighborhoods filled
with those of us in witness protection,
a brief smile and wave to our neighbors
before locking all the doors.

The false leniency of my sentence
after confessing my sins.
Rote prayers without any consequence
but the visual of me kneeling
in repentance in public
without a behavior change.

No statute of limitation exists
under the harsh white light
of conscience, mentally flipping
through the thick book of pages
filled with people whom I harmed
through silence & confess:
I could have been a better man.

Hard-Won Peace

Under a cloudless sky,
A dying brown-spotted,
Leaf-yellowed European beech
Casts an ink blot shadow
On the green sheet of lawn,
Separating in the wind into
Tendrils of lines, reminding me
I have thank you letters
To write, receiving condolences
After my father's death.

Funnel cloud of autumn leaves
On the patio like a child spinning,
Giddy from being off balance.
The laughter of my daughter
In another room of the house.
Twelve out of fifty-six years here.
Three cats, now one puppy and one cat.
Empty circle of chairs staged
Around the fire pit. All that is lost,
Yes, but also what still remains.

IV.

The Anti-Heroic Couplet
of Alternative Endings

Old newspaper clippings,
Black and white photos
Of a former girlfriend hidden
Inside a nondescript book,
Cleaning my father's house
After he died, yellowed
And desiccating, wondering
If he wanted it to be found
Before it perished unseen.
Not aiming for metaphor
Or laboring as an arcane semiotician,
But perhaps just wanting me
To know there was once a time
He laughed with abandon,
When alcohol encouraged him
To be a bon vivant rather than
The cliché of a broken man.
Flipping through memories
Like old family scrapbooks,
Knowing I would not have existed
If he had lived a different life.
The past narratives we must learn to bury
Trying to live beyond regret and fury.

How Hope Births Its Way into the Body

Distant sirens remind us
there is another emergency,
a good Samaritan keeps
a victim from dying alone,

while across the street
from an urban clinic,
a bus stop bench advertises
free Narcan if you scan a QR code.

Inside, a physician failing to keep
on schedule due to so much need
sits across from an unshaven man
with a stained T- shirt who admits

he is still intermittently using
crack cocaine. How to convey
a stare that connotates concern
and empathy from a voice

imperceptibly breaking at the end of
"Is there anything I can do to help?"
A two-minute dramatic monologue
of tragedy: just released from jail,

home eviction, son dead
of an overdose, and the accumulating
organs beginning to fail.
Through the detritus of words

they scavenge through
they rescue "*we*," "*help*,"
"*come back*," and the next day
he returns. Needles, syringes,

alcohol pads, he carefully rubs
his skin, the pad wiping up
grime and sweat, watching
insulin now slowly tunnel

into his skin, and no one
who witnesses him outside
today will know how hope
births its way into the body.

The Symbolism of Suburban Deer

A fawn traipses through a suburban backyard,
a supermarket of clover and dandelions,
her mother a few paces behind, a helicopter
parent no longer anxious about walking through
what was once an open field where previous
generations had to fear the smell of cordite
if they didn't eat with their ears fully alert
for a broken twig and the split-second
head start Nature gave them to escape.
How many of them would prefer the past?
Supposedly closer to the capstone of Maslow's
Hierarchy of Needs, we have become too timid
after burying our influences, our name
a nonce word as the author of a poem
entering the universe waiting for someone
to notice that words like atoms exist to fissure
into consciousness: "*Let there be light*,"
and you let faith become a part of you.
The world dying for an armistice of words
with a fidelity that reaches the hardest of hearing.

Writing Prompt

Decades now of this walk
where a canopy of oaks
conceals winter's abandoned
birds' nests. Wind rushing
through a field of fescue,
catching a glimpse of white clover
like the hemline of a girl's dress
before the image disappears.
A playground sits empty,
no starker antonym to describe
the presence versus the absence
of children on a swing or slide.
Knee and hip pain, early warning
system of an upcoming storm.
Bless the mind, a never-quit coach
saying there is still a chance to win.
Well-stocked pharmacy of salicin
in the bark of a lone Black willow,
how it has to undergo oxidation,
a process of loss before acting
as a pain reliever, taking a break
before you get back out there.

In These Times

Waking hours, anxious sky
turning from cigarette ash
to electric stove coil color,
where the tea kettle whistle heralds
another late-night of the mind
working overtime wandering
the landscape of consciousness,
confronting past trauma,
current struggles, and future unknowns,
everyone gowned and gloved,
waiting on you to perform
a lifesaving triple bypass,
and you can't even stand
the sight of blood.
Unexpectedly, the thought
of hoping the traffic
is sparse on Main Street
for an urban dwelling bird
ecstatically pecking at a piece of bread,
satiated at least for tonight,
or a flock of birds
weathering the pain of rain
striking their wings across
rural farms, fearlessly flying
between wood openings
of a church's roof,
housing in temporary shelter
until the storm passes.
Realizing you have overlooked
the ingenuity of birds.

In Admiration of the Believers

I remember the intimidating
heavy wooden doors
and the severe austerity
standing in the narthex,
yet welcoming everyone
in its capaciousness.
Even the stray pigeon
transfixed by the kaleidoscope
of colors from a stained-glass window
panel depicting the crucifixion of Jesus.

I am estranged from my faith.
Rilke's plea of whom would hear
his cries among the angelic orders
can be answered, "*No one,*"
even if astronauts were able
to scream his poetry
from the heavens since sound
waves can't travel through space.
But I abhor the arrogance
of atheists who quote Einstein.

It is not insanity to see
the infirm struggling to kneel
every Sunday convinced
their suffering will be ameliorated.
Spiritually laughing at the drugs
and procedures that aim to stave off
death for what is a drop of time

in the immense bucket of eternity.
Empiricism put in its place
by the inviolable fraternity of believers.

The strength of citizens fighting
fire with fire, gathering on a Spring night
outside the Notre Dame Cathedral
for a candlelight vigil after
its wooden spire was engulfed in flames.
Watching it be rebuilt
like a controlled burn
maintaining the health of the faithful,
even more sure their belief
can't be incinerated by elemental forces.

If You Feel You Have Wasted Your Life, Then Read This Poem

The first time you feel
pain in a hip or knee
and know it won't heal
with ice, meds, or time,
is when the calendar
of autumn is approaching.
Chlorophyll breaking down
during the shortening days,
first appearance of orange
and yellow, and if there is
enough sugar in the leaves,
streaks of red will make
even the jaded take notice.
At risk now during self-reflection,
the inventory of mistakes
threatens to overwhelm
the storage capacity of the mind.
Nicotine-dependence listed
on your medical chart,
but you never smoked the cigar
given to you on your child's birth.
Alcohol-dependent as well,
you never opened the bottle
of gifted bourbon, either.
Regrets like the sadness
of knowing you will only have
a few days left of hearing children
laugh outdoors during recess.

I want you to think of my father
increasing the flow of oxygen
as high as it could just to get up
and move from the couch
to the floor to play with
his preschool granddaughter,
mesmerized by a large container
filled with buttons of various sizes
smiling at him with such joy
it made the necessity of saving
them through the years
because of poverty feel worth it,
like gifting her a treasure
of gold coins she still remembers
five years after his death.

One Tree Hill

A developer gestures
    with his hands
to a prospective client,
    the sea reflected
in both their sunglasses,
    while a solitary
limbo gumbo tree remains
    recalcitrantly dug into
a seaside hill.
    A solitary flycatcher
lands and grips
    a question mark-shaped branch
the circumference of a pencil,
    scribbling furiously now
from a gust of wind
    before adding its voice
for good measure.
    I append these words
to register my solidarity
    in protest to the dominant
gradient of blue
    that captures everyone's attention
from shore to horizon,
    razing nature to denominations
of banknote green
    and the sound of waves
that overwhelms the century-long
    susurration of windswept leaves.

If the Nobel Prize Winners of Medicine and Peace had a Conversation

Even healers use the word *elimination*,
marshaling strategic plans to attack
a roundworm that has disrupted
the homeostasis of the body, a parasite
that represents a threat to be vigilant against.
Elsewhere, curious eyes observe
a one-millimeter roundworm with *elegans*
in its scientific name and discover
an almost invisible courier of information
that influences the difference between
a cell's optimal function and malfunction.
On this rain-drenched day that washes
earthworms on my driveway, I research
the relationship between earthworms
and roundworms and discover they have
less in common than I thought, falling
under the immense category of invertebrates.
Still, I gently pick up the earthworms
And move them to my lawn, creating pockets
Of air, giving the roots room to spread.

A Retired Physician
Rediscovers Wonder

A career spent attending to others,
unworldly and seemingly devoid
of any hobbies or great adventures.
For decades you would solemnly
listen to your patients' heart and lungs,
a long-married couple sharing a house
but sleeping in separate rooms,
trying to make sense
of what its owner was feeling
and what you heard,

sometimes quashing hopes
of distant plans when reality
counseled a shortened calendar.
The romance of grandly traveling
the world now has to settle
for tentatively navigating a few steps.
Upstairs and downstairs cordoned off,
a lifetime of curated exhibits
no longer relevant
to the current patron's diminished mien.

Daily mood of ever-present anxiety,
wondering what could go wrong
with each patient under your care.
Staying with many of them until the lights
went out and they vacated
the body's home. Sometimes downplaying
and minimizing accumulating deficits,
they would call you like a handyman
hoping you could somehow prolong
body parts that don't come with a warranty.

The labs, studies, and phone calls
are someone else's responsibility
you think, startled by an inpatient driver's horn,
driving home in the summer twilight
in awe of the surrounding grasses,
trees, clouds, and stars that you never bothered
to learn more about, committing to take a class
with the professors of wonder-
elementary school children-
learning about local wetlands you didn't know existed
and what other discoveries await these last years.

How Revolutions Begin

Midwestern nice, he reminds himself,
while listening to overbearing parents
brag about their children, who like him
hope their future debts and obligations
are fixed rather than compounded,
before starting his fourteen-hour
drive home, marveling at the queue
forming to ride a Ferris wheel
in a department store in Fargo, North Dakota.
Driving past Iverson Lake
in Otter Tail County, Minnesota
while watching two western Grebes
in flight writing cursively on the Nile Blue
sheet of a Sunday afternoon sky without
any apparent urgency, he pulls off
the highway in quiet protest to itineraries
and watches a dragonfly puncture
the glass mirror lake, thinking this is how
revolutions begin, by upsetting the status quo.

Chaos Theory

Stalled engine, leaking antifreeze,
pulled off the side of a highway
near midnight on a Friday in January
driving through rural Pennsylvania,
moon illuminating the landscape
like an x-ray. Two hours left
of an eight-hour drive before attending
to the busyness of a dying father.
Drawback of a life spent under
desk lamps instead of car hoods,
thinking of sending a thank you card
to the engineer who designed
the translucent coolant reservoir
for those of us who haven't read
The Complete Idiot's Guide
to What's Under a Car Hood.

No Proustian or Stoic-like epiphanies
while confined to a prison cell-like room,
sentenced to hard labor of breathing.
As a young boy, I wanted to catch a butterfly
flitting through a small patch of wildflowers
until my father explained pollination.
Letting it go, unsure if other butterflies
would return and contribute color
and beauty to a dying manufacturing town.
All the lawyers, doctors, nurses,
bill collectors and aides, trying to stack
sandbags on a low-lying island
before a once-in-a lifetime typhoon
strike from the flight path
a butterfly took all those years ago.

Our Insignificance
is Still with Immensity

"... A year later, /repotting Michiko's avocado, I find/a long black hair tangled in the dirt."

Jack Gilbert, "Married"

I stood on the roadside grass
Looking up at the Wyoming sky,
Late middle-age, transfixed
By a Western Meadowlark
In flight and thought of Jack Gilbert
Finding a single strand of his wife's hair
A year after her death.
The negative capability
Of discovering that my height
Is smaller in comparison
To the Kármán Line than a human
Hair is to a six-foot-tall human
Didn't last, thinking of Darwin
And later generations of ground finches
Whose beaks can extract seeds
And nuts a little easier avoiding
Extinction. Matins and vespers
Are absent from the birdsong canon.
Closer to earth, I observed the chaos
Of a swallowtail flapping its wings
On that August day and give praise
Without prayer five years later
To someone who will wake up today
And decide it's time to change his life.

Turing Test

I typed my poem in a search engine
After being inspired by Rilke's
"Who, if I cried out, would hear me
Among the angels' hierarchies?",
And in less than a second
I got the following response:
"It looks like there aren't any great
Matches for your search."
Mic-drop tech evangelists,
Believing the Information Age
Will answer
Our most pressing searches.

Ornithographies

after the photography of Xavi Bou
Harnessed and banded with technology
the jackdaw becomes less mysterious
in flight, no longer believed to announce
a birth when landing on a roof or heralding
a death nesting in a chimney. Fact-
checked folklore and the accumulating opus
of scientific literature reducing every act
to the survival of the fittest. What narratives
exist in rereading the calligraphy of wings
scrawling across the Nile Blue sheet of sky
knowing its family is safe from predation,
their hunger sated, & the viewer experiencing
wonder again in every invisible commute
recorded from departure to destination.

Almost Negative Capability

Well into the age of diminishment
Ruminating over the sound
Of car wheels doing a K-turn
In a gravel lot after a friend's burial.
Any new visual or hearing insights
Long mothballed in the mind's attic.
Subtraction of the world to this:
Walking to the pond as if getting up from
Being tackled by an entire football team.
Still the choice of elegy or ecstasy.
Lingering late autumnal leaves
Scampering through windswept grass
Before jumping blindly and landing
In the water or temporarily stymied
By the khaki-colored leaves of cattails
And their abundant cob flower spikes.
Quiet determination to see another spring
When the leaves turn to emerald green
And the wind plays through them, sound
Of a drum brush concluding a ballad
Just as the diaphanous wings
Of a dragonfly hover a few feet away,
Waning sun putting you under the spotlight.

Coda

It is not that life is meaningless
even though our names may be written on water.
Tomes of knowledge found under the night sky.
Devotion to empiricism,
deliberately ignorant of the gods
no matter the harshness of circumstances.
Late night vigils over the body
with parts that don't come with a warranty.
Aging begins to turn us into apparitions,
silently nodding to the ghosts,
experiencing the burning of days.
Late middle age, transfixed
by the sun's rays like watch hands
and the resonance of what remains,
waning sun putting you under the spotlight.

NOTES

"Ghazal for the Sleepless Children": The word "Hayati," used as a child's name, means "my life" in Arabic.

"Sorry for Your Loss": "...Because we will never be/ what the field remembers," is from "Leaving the Field," by Sophie Cabot Black.

"STEM As Part of a Flower": "blushful Hippocrene" is from "Ode to a Nightingale" by John Keats.

"Obituaries of the Anonymous": Researchers collected 70,716 individual specimens from bird-building collisions in Chicago, Illinois from 1978-2016. M. Zimova, B.C. Weeks, D.E. Willard, S.T. Giery, V. Jirinec, R.C. Burner, & B.M. Winger, Body size predicts the rate of contemporary morphological change in birds, Proc. Natl. Acad. Sci. U.S.A. 120 (20) e2206971120, https://doi.org/10.1073/pnas.2206971120 (2023).

"Vigil": The line, "Every real intimacy includes its end." is from "Zero at the Bone," by Christian Wiman.

"Coda": Created from individual lines of poems in the book. The first and last lines of the poem are the first and last lines of the book.

Acknowledgments

Grateful acknowledgment is made to the editors of the following journals where these poems were first published, sometimes in an earlier version:

Annals of Internal Medicine: "Self-Reflection on an Elevated BMI"

As It Ought To Be Magazine: "STEM As Part of a Flower"

Book of Matches: "On Overhearing a Conversation about Momma Bears"

Broad River Review: "Liminality"

The Calendula Review: "Pediatric Psychiatric Crisis Center Located on Butterfly Garden Drive, Columbus, Ohio," "Vigil"

Chiron Review: "Being Called Soft as a Boy"

Cloudbank: "Almost Negative Capability," "How Revolutions Begin"

The Dodge: "What I Hope My Daughter Learns"

The Dolomite Review: "Ornithographies"

Four Tulips: "The Resonance of Seashells," "One Tree Hill"

The Ekphrastic Review: "The Subversion of Michelangelo"

Ionosphere: "The Misuse of Data"

Ivo Review: "If You Feel You Have Wasted Your Life, Then Read This Poem"

JAMA (Journal of the American Medical Association): "House Call"

North Dakota Quarterly: "The Rising Price of Oranges," The Last Shall Be First," "What We Miss from Our Grandmothers"

The Pharos: "A Retired Physician Rediscovers Wonder"

Pictura Journal: "In Praise of the Common Yarrow"

Poets for Science: "Obituaries of the Anonymous"

Qu: "Coming Up Sevens"

Rawhead: A Journal of Art and Literature: "Time to Say Goodbye," "Chaos Theory," "Failing Better"

Red Branch Review: "Still Life With Oranges"

Santa Barbara Literary Journal: "Potential Energy"

Schuylkill Valley Journal: "Anyone Can Be Successful If They Try Hard Enough," "The Mercy of Migration"

The Scop: "Philosophy of the Quick Brown Fox," "Childhood"

The Soliloquist: "Our Insignificance Is Still With Immensity," "Hard-Won Peace"

St. Katherine Review: "Getting Older"

Stone Poetry Quarterly: "If the Nobel Prize Winners of Medicine and Peace had a Conversation"

Talking River Review: "Sunday Mornings"

wildscape. literary journal: "Marshmallow Test"

THE AUTHOR

Vigil is Joseph Geskey's second book of poems. His first, *Alms for the Ravens,* was published in 2024. His poetry has appeared in *Verse Daily, JAMA, Poetry East, Tar River Poetry, The Dodge,* and many other literary journals. He has been nominated twice for a Pushcart Prize. A physician who practices in an underserved area of Columbus, Ohio, he lives in Dublin, Ohio with his wife and daughter.